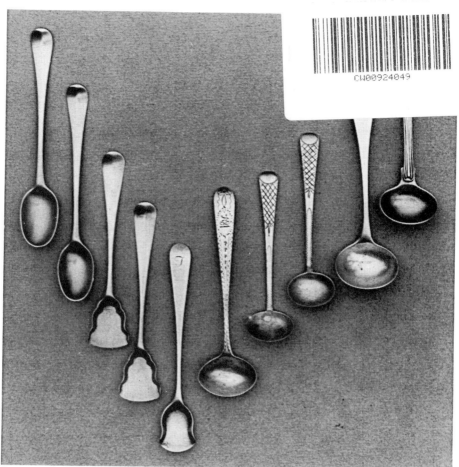

A group of condiment spoons: (left to right) two long-handled mustard spoons, about 1750; two Hanoverian and one Old English salt shovel, about 1740-60; Irish bright-cut decorated Old English pattern salt spoon, about 1780; two cross-hatch engraved Old English salt spoons (Birmingham), 1804; plain Old English salt spoon, 1825; fiddle and thread salt spoon, 1802.

SPOONS
1650-1930

Simon Moore

Shire Publications Ltd

CONTENTS

Copyright © 1987 by Simon Moore. First published 1987. Shire Album 211. ISBN 0 85263 910 4.

Set in 9 point Times roman and printed in Great Britain by C. I. Thomas & Sons (Haverfordwest) Ltd, Press Buildings, Merlins Bridge, Haverfordwest, Dyfed.

British Library Cataloguing in Publication Data available.

ACKNOWLEDGEMENTS
The author offers his thanks to those who have kindly helped in providing material for illustration: the British Museum; the Victoria and Albert Museum (especially Miranda Poliakoff); Temple Newsam House Museum, Leeds; Bill Brown; Sanda Lipton; Leslie Spatt. He also expresses his gratitude to Christies, Phillips and Sothebys, and especially to those whose expertise, patience and advice have helped him with the text — Helen Bennell and Martin Gubbins. Photographs are acknowledged as follows: Christies, pages 4 (left), 24; Phillips, pages 5 (bottom left), 6 (left), 7, 11 (bottom left), 14 (right), 21 (bottom left); Sothebys, pages 9, 14; Temple Newsam House, Leeds, page 13 (top). All other photographs are by the author, taken by courtesy of: the British Museum, page 2; Sanda Lipton, pages 1, 5 (top and bottom far right), 18 (top), 21 (top); London Company of Pewterers, page 12; Vivika, Chenil Galleries, London, page 29 (bottom left); Victoria and Albert Museum, pages 4 (centre), 10, 15, 22. All other plates are by courtesy of private collectors.

COVER: *A selection of silver and gilt spoons from 1652 to 1927. (From bottom left, moving right and upwards) Rococo salt shovel, gilt teaspoon with cherub and lyre, mote skimmer, all about 1750. Inscribed Puritan spoon by Steven Venables, 1652. Engraved gilt trefid spoon by Lawrence Coles, 1683. Dognose tablespoon by Edward Gibson, 1704. Rococo tablespoon by Jeremiah Lee, 1733. Bacchanalian gilt dessert spoon by William Theobalds, 1834. Vine-pattern dessert spoon by William Theobalds, 1837. Late art nouveau spoon by JSR, Birmingham, 1927. (Upper section, right to left) Two art nouveau teaspoons, 1902, (the one on the right is by William Comyns; the one on the left a superb enamelled spoon, one of the Liberty's 'Cymric' range designed by Archibald Knox). Irish Hanoverian mustard spoon, about 1770. Rococo teaspoon with mask, about 1750.*

BELOW: *Two silver spoons of Roman form, engraved 'Saulos' and 'Paulos', from the Sutton Hoo treasure, seventh century AD.*

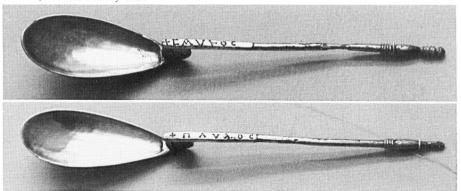

An assortment of medieval and sixteenth-century knopped spoons on an eighteenth-century spoon rack. The top row are all of pewter: (left to right) two acorn-knopped spoons, diamond point, baluster, twisted ball (wrythen) and a sixteenth-century melon knop. Bottom row (left to right): latten cone knop, pewter stylised acorn, two pewter maidenhead knops — that on the left wearing a horned headdress (atours) which was fashionable in the mid fifteenth century, a silver seal-top (1592) with town mark struck in the bowl and an early sixteenth-century latten slip-top.

EARLY HISTORY

Spoons have always been popular as gifts; apart from the more usual occasions such as christenings, they have been given as tokens of love and faith at weddings and as memorials at funerals. In previous centuries they were treasured since, like knives, they were an essential of ordinary life and so were carried by everyone.

Spoons have been popular as collectors' items since Victorian times; they are small, useful and often inexpensive, and their history is long and interesting. Styles varied in popularity and some were affected by historical events.

Man's first attempts at making spoons were crude by modern standards, but effective: the end of a bone or antler was scooped out or a shell was tied on to a stick. Throughout the bronze and iron ages people continued to use such materials although a few spoons made from a copper alloy such as bronze have been found. Iron was impractical as a spoon-making metal.

Following the Roman invasion a large number of more sophisticated and better balanced spoons were introduced to Britain. They were made from bone, pewter, bronze and silver. The earliest examples of the spoon (*cochlear* in Latin) comprised a round bowl attached to a *stele* (narrow handle) that tapered down to a spike. The spike was used for spearing snails from their shells. Later Roman spoons show the incorporation of an elbow into the design while the bowl became either purse-shaped or pear-shaped. By the second or third century AD another spoon design had appeared, characterised by a coiled handle and a larger bowl. It was probably used for supping liquids and resembles the spoons used by the Egyptians as mixing bowls for applying cosmetics rather than eating. During the fifth century Roman power in Britain crumbled but spoons still conformed to Roman design, as evidenced by those found in the Sutton Hoo ship burial.

The more outlandish culture brought by Saxon and Viking invaders soon altered the classic Roman spoon design to a broader and leaf-shaped bowl attached by a zoomorphic (animal's head) junction to a long stele. Medieval spoon bowls were rounded into a fig shape and the steles were ornamented with small decorative knobs known as *knops*. Spoon knops were at first either of acorn shape or abstract form such as lozenge (diamond), baluster or ball, sometimes twisted, known as *wrythen*. Later medieval spoons and those produced during the Tudor period show how the popularity of knops continued as spoon-makers adorned their wares with anthropomorphic and zoomorphic knops. The *maidenhead knop*, normally coifed with a period headdress, was the earliest of figural knops, others being the *lion sejant* or sitting lion and the *apostle*. The apostle's head was capped with a small disc (nimbus) which represented his halo and he carried an identifying emblem which was often the instrument of his martyrdom.

Spoons were given as christening gifts because, like other eating implements, they were not supplied at table and therefore everyone carried their own. Social status was reflected in the type of spoon carried. Apostle spoons were especially popular as christening gifts, with the child's patron saint on top of the spoon's stele. Sometimes they were made in sets of thirteen, representing the twelve apostles with the addition of Christ as the thirteenth. Towards the end of the sixteenth century the baluster knop was capped with a disc similar to the

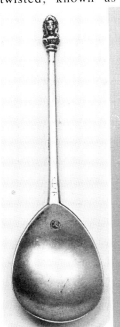   

(Left to right) A silver maidenhead-knop spoon by John Eydes of Exeter, about 1580. Lion sejant spoon, about 1530, and the lion enlarged. An apostle spoon of St Simon Zelotes, 1578.

4

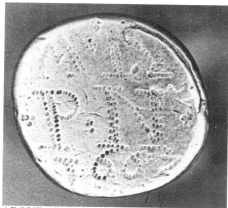

ABOVE: *Top view of seal-top spoon knop with pricked inscription 'AN/PN/1667'. Probably presented to a couple on the occasion of their marriage.*

apostle's nimbus. This arrangement, known as a *seal-top*, was also popular since the initials of the owner and donor could be pricked or engraved on to the disc rather than the stele. Knops for silver spoons were cast separately, attached to the stele by a soldered joint and then gilded. The assay office marks were struck on the back of the stele with the exception of the town mark, which was struck in the bowl.

Knopped spoons continued to be made during the first half of the seventeenth century, the apostle and seal-top being the most popular. The apostle knops, however, became cruder as the moulds for casting them began to wear out and the spoons were heavier and clumsier to use.

In contrast to the more elaborately

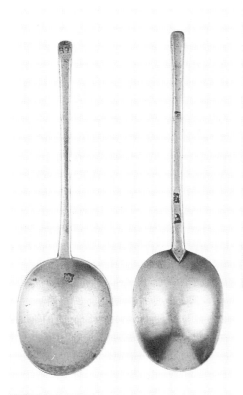

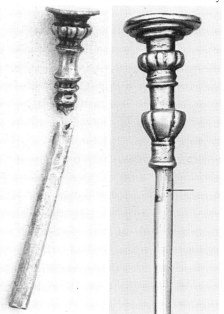

ABOVE: *Solder joints for knops. (Left) A detached London seal-top showing a characteristic 'V' join. (Right) A seal-top spoon knop showing a stepped join (darker solder line arrowed) used by provincial makers (Norwich in this instance).*

LEFT: *Pair of Commonwealth slip-top spoons by William Cary of London. The date letter mark for 1653 has been lifted to discourage the addition of a knop after hallmarking.*

knopped spoons, the *slip-top* was made for people of simpler tastes, but not necessarily less well-off as many were made in silver as well as in pewter and latten (brass). The slip-top was easy to produce and could be cheap (10d per half gross for pewter in 1580). The end of the stele was cut through at an angle, leaving the handle unadorned. The slip-top spoon, already used since the later fifteenth century by those who preferred plainer pieces of silver, underwent a popular revival during Charles I's reign since its plain appearance was more appealing to puritanical taste than its more elaborate contemporaries. A pewter counterpart was produced in large numbers during the later sixteenth and early seventeenth centuries. The simpler appearance of the slip-top might account for its present comparative scarcity since many were resold for melt or, if made of pewter, were thrown away as they wore out or were broken.

Some less scrupulous goldsmiths appear to have tried adding a knop after the assaying of a silver slip-top spoon, to avoid paying more for the assay. The position of the date letter mark was consequently moved near the top of the stele of slip-top spoons in order to prevent such cheating, since the subsequent addition of a knop would have melted away or disfigured such a mark. This practice was continued during the Commonwealth.

Positioning of silver hallmarks. (Left to right) Trefid spoon, 1693, showing the town mark (arrowed) now moved alongside the other hallmarks, which are more evenly spaced; later eighteenth-century spoon showing marks for 1778 close together on the reverse of the stem; and a rare set for 1781 before they were moved.

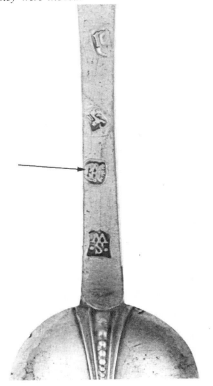

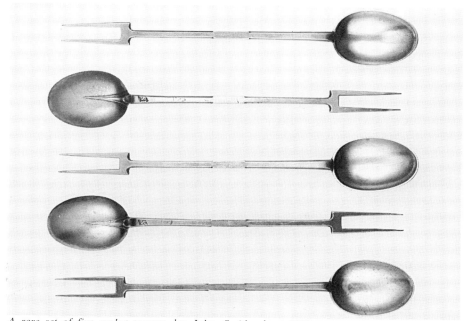

A rare set of five sucket spoons by John Smith, about 1685.

COMMONWEALTH SPOONS

With the ascendancy of Cromwell and Puritanism, spoons of earlier styles with religious knops fell into disfavour since they smacked of popery. Some apparently had their apostle knops forcibly removed and could be distinguished from the simpler lines of the now popular slip-top spoon only by the latter spoon's thickened terminal. Not many slip-top spoons were made at this time, however, because a totally new type of spoon was produced.

With its flattened stele, completely unadorned, and its heavy elliptical bowl, the aptly named *puritan spoon* was the first spoon to show any substantial change in design for about five hundred years. It was evidently popular since many were made during the Commonwealth period both in silver and in base metal. Those made from latten were subsequently tinned as the metal would otherwise taint food, especially if it had

been prepared with vinegar. Spoons that were tinned were marked with the normal spoonmaker's mark of his initials and surrounded by the words DOUBLE WHYTED, indicating that the spoon had been twice sealed with molten tin. Many who made spoons in latten produced more adventurous punches to mark their wares. Some of the resulting touchmarks consisted of the maker's initials with one or several contemporary spoons in miniature and so clearly delineated that one can still recognise them as puritan, slip-top or seal-top.

Sometime during the Commonwealth the first post-medieval *sucket spoons* (a spoon at one end, a fork at the other) were made; the basic design resembles that of two Saxon sucket spoons found at Sevington in Wiltshire. Commonwealth sucket spoons usually show the stamp of puritan plainness. Some were made in sets of six but few seem to have survived.

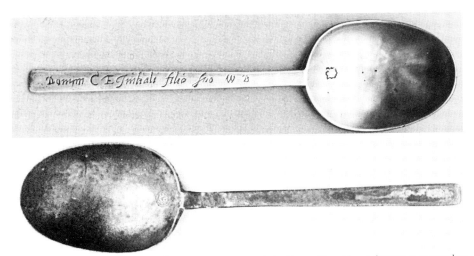

Commonwealth puritan spoons: the upper one was made by Steven Venables, a famous spoonmaker of London. The handle bears the inscription (translated) 'The gift of C.E. Tintial to his son W.B.' The lower spoon has been made from latten subsequently tinned.

The forked end was used in the manner of earlier forks for eating sticky sweetmeats. Sucket spoons were not accepted as part of the eventual table trio of knife, fork and spoon, which began to be used together only during the late seventeenth century.

Another sweetmeat-associated spoon was made during the Commonwealth period although its origin can be traced back to the beginning of the seventeenth century. It was designed to dip into a table spice box which stood on short silver legs and was normally shaped like a

A spoonmaker's mark in the bowl of a tinned latten apostle spoon, about 1670, comprising 'L R' in a circle of dots and three seal-top spoons.

8

cockle shell. The spoon bowl was either oval or slightly pointed at the front. The short and wavy stele, similar to Roman 'swan-handled spoons', ended in a horse's hoof terminal. It is known as a *hoof spoon,* not to be confused with the rarer spoon from the same period with a knop shaped like a horse's hoof but with a normal straight stele and fig-shaped bowl.

Puritan spoons were sometimes filed with one, two or three notches at the top of the handle. The reason for this simple decoration is not known. It has also been noted on the handle of the earliest known English silver fork (1632) and occasionally on spoons as late as 1670. The notches may have been a precursor of the new-styled terminal that appeared during the Restoration period on spoons and later on forks.

Three rare spice-box spoons; early to mid seventeenth century.

9

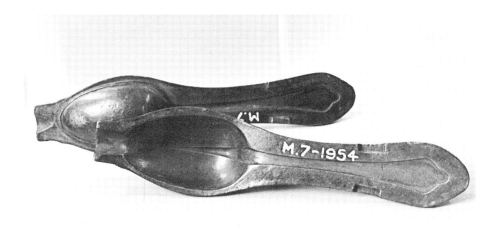

Bronze mould for dognose spoons, early eighteenth century.

THE LATER SEVENTEENTH CENTURY

With the restoration of the monarchy in 1660 sacred and fancy knops came back into favour and some older styles of knopped spoons were revived. The puritan spoon design was still popular and was quickly modified to fit in with the changing fashion, the *trefid spoon* evolving directly from it. Its terminal was broadened and either formed into three lobes or filed with two notches, giving the appearance of a cloven hoof, which is why it is sometimes also known as *pied de biche*. The spoonmakers also lengthened the peg, where the bowl meets the handle, into a tapering support known as a *rat-tail* (also found on the reverse of some Roman spoon bowls) running longitudinally underneath the bowl.

The back of the bowl and the front of the spoon handle were sometimes embossed with a swirling design known as *lacework,* which was either carved into the spoon mould or template or else subsequently chased on to the spoon. Other spoons were lavishly engraved all over with foliage, the rat-tail support forming the rib of an engraved acanthus leaf under the bowl. The traditional town mark was moved from the bowl to the reverse of the handle with the other assay marks, since a hard blow struck in the bowl by the assayer's punch would have

dented the rat-tail.

Silver trefid spoons were made by the traditional forging method of hammering out each end of an ingot into a rough spoon shape. The centre of the bowl's reverse was left untreated, leaving a raised tapering area for forming the rat-tail. The handle was hammered along both edges to give it strength and the bowl was dished into a lead template. The spoon surface was then planished. The stele to bowl junction was hammered against a rod-shaped anvil to form an angle and the end of the handle (terminal) was turned up in a similar manner. Finally the spoon was filed to the desired shape and polished.

During the later seventeenth century spoons were sometimes cast in moulds. The molten metal was poured into the pre-heated mould, usually made from bronze, and when it had cooled slightly the spoon was removed, the sprue (waste) was cut off and the spoon was finished with file, planishing hammer and polish. Base-metal examples were nearly always cast and the moulds were sometimes carved with ornamentation or a special commemorative design. One of the most famous of these spoon designs was made to commemorate the coronation of Queen Anne.

RIGHT: *A range of trefid spoons showing a variety of terminals. The back of the bowl (left) has been ornamented with lacework.*

BELOW: *Reverse of three trefid spoons showing one plain and two beaded rat-tail bowl supports.*
BELOW RIGHT: *Both sides of a silver-gilt trefid spoon by Lawrence Coles, London, 1683, with acanthus engraving and an entire leaf surrounding the rat-tail on the reverse of the bowl.*

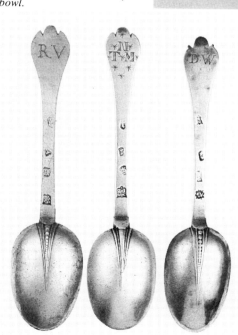

11

Base-metal spoons were also made by itinerant spoonmakers, whose less well finished products can occasionally be found. Such a spoonmaker would have carried a set of alphabetical stamps so that a purchaser's initials could be hammered into the spoon. Initials were usually engraved into silver, often in a triangle, the upper letter being the surname initial.

Whereas spoons had previously been used for eating all manner of food, two smaller-sized spoons appeared during the 'trefid period' (about 1660-1710). The earliest tea and dessert spoons were made as smaller versions of the tablespoon, which previously had a universal function and which was now reserved for soup. Many tea and dessert spoons were similarly decorated with foliate engraving according to the fashion of the period.

Another type of spoon which was engraved in like manner was the much less common *folding spoon,* revived at this time. English examples are particularly rare. There is one medieval diamond-point spoon, found at Scarborough, which has been hinged at the base of the stele. A sliding collar shaped like a Saxon helmet can be moved over the hinged section to lock the spoon in an open position. During the trefid spoon period a few silversmiths made folding spoons and forks hinged at the bowl to stele junction. A movable collar was added which slides down the stele over a small silver tongue attached to the bowl so that the spoon (or fork) could be locked open.

After a long period of disfavour table forks began to be accepted and (about 1680) were made singly or in sets of six or twelve, as also were spoons. Together spoons and forks have become known as *flatware* (as opposed to *hollow ware* — beakers and other vessels for the table).

Spoonmakers all over Britain produced many more spoons than previously. In the West Country particularly, there were goldsmiths working in many towns and, rather than being sent for assay at

LEFT: *Pewter dognose spoons commemorating the coronation of Queen Anne in 1702.* RIGHT: *Close-up of the middle spoon's terminal.*

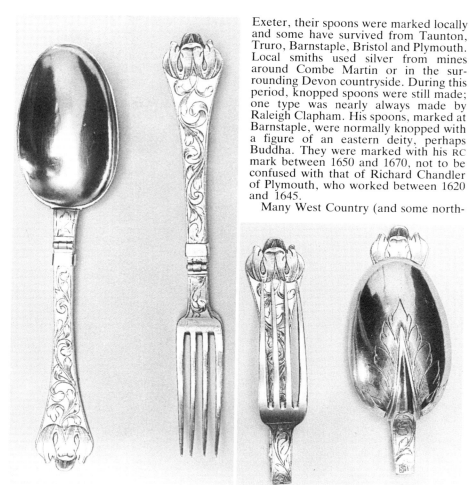

Exeter, their spoons were marked locally and some have survived from Taunton, Truro, Barnstaple, Bristol and Plymouth. Local smiths used silver from mines around Combe Martin or in the surrounding Devon countryside. During this period, knopped spoons were still made; one type was nearly always made by Raleigh Clapham. His spoons, marked at Barnstaple, were normally knopped with a figure of an eastern deity, perhaps Buddha. They were marked with his RC mark between 1650 and 1670, not to be confused with that of Richard Chandler of Plymouth, who worked between 1620 and 1645.

Many West Country (and some north-

ABOVE: *Engraved folding trefid spoon and fork, shown extended (left) and folded (right).*

BELOW: *Broad-ended trefid spoon, the almost puritan-shaped bowl stamped with the town mark of Exeter, about 1670.*

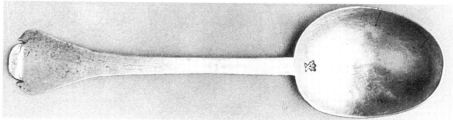

ern) trefid spoons were characterised by a broadly splayed trefid end and others were additionally decorated with chased circles on the stele. In the north of England and in Scotland spoon handles were also chased with circles and capped with disc finials — a characteristic Scottish feature since the later sixteenth century. A few examples were engraved with a skull and sobering inscriptions such as THINK ON or LIVE TO DIE and DIE TO LIVE, showing that people were still as obsessed with mortality as their medieval ancestors. These spoons were sometimes engraved with the name of the deceased and given as a memorial to relatives at funerals, perhaps also as gloomy reminders of their own inevitable death.

Some spoons of the trefid period and later were made with narrower handles which were scooped out along one side so that they could be used for extracting marrow from bones prepared especially for this purpose. Eventually the taste for marrow became so popular that by the mid eighteenth century two-ended scoops were being made to accompany the usual service of flatware. The fashion continued into the early nineteenth century and a few silver-plated examples were made for those with lesser means, but very few seem to have been made in base metal, presumably as those who could not afford the luxury of silver were not interested in owning a spoon made for the sole purpose of eating bone marrow.

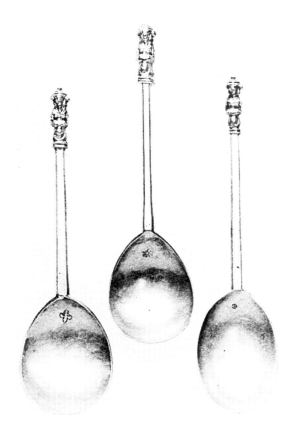

LEFT: *Three West Country Buddha-knop spoons, about 1660.* BELOW: *The mark of Raleigh Clapham, Barnstaple.*

14

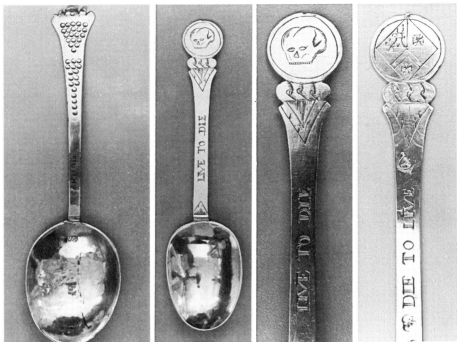

ABOVE FAR LEFT: *A West Country spoon characteristically chased with circles, dated 1679.*
ABOVE RIGHT: *(From left) York 'memento mori' spoon by Thomas Mangy, 1670; the disc end engraved with a skull and (far right) a woman's coat of arms; along the stele, 'Live to Die/Die to Live'.*
BELOW: *(From top) Marrow spoon by Thomas Issod, 1695, engraved with acanthus decoration; marrow spoon by William Petley, 1718; two-ended marrow scoop with beaded stele, by George Smith and William Fearn, 1788.*

Comparison of Old English flatware with contemporary cutlery (about 1770), showing which side up they would have been laid on the table (excepting the tiny snuff spoon). Included are bright-cut engraved tablespoons and teaspoons (in dish and tea saucer) and a feather-edged tablespoon (along top).

THE EARLY EIGHTEENTH CENTURY

At the end of the seventeenth century the trefid spoon began to be displaced by a new style, the trefid notches disappearing, leaving the central part of the terminal standing alone. This wavy end is usually known as *dognose* (it faintly resembles a hound's head) although it is sometimes called *shield-top*. The dognose spoon prevailed throughout the reign of Queen Anne and is occasionally called a 'Queen Anne spoon'. The flattened trefid-style handle narrowed and became more rounded in section. The bowl was still supported with a rat-tail but was more elongated than the trefid and the spoon started to resemble the design used today. Spoonmakers preferred to make some of their spoons without dognose ends, as these were rather uncomfortable to hold, and produced just a plainly rounded terminal, which, like the trefid and dognose spoons, turned up at the

end. The new-styled handle also embodied a central spine of metal running longitudinally from the terminal to the narrow shaft of the spoon. These changes in design increased in popularity so that by the time of George I's accession in 1714 the new pattern was fast becoming accepted as the standard and has been nicknamed *Hanoverian*.

Around 1715 the rat-tail was gradually superseded by a much shorter strengthening known as a *drop*, which took several different forms — the double drop and the sometimes extended single drop. The two overlapped each other for about thirty years. From this period silver flatware was acquired by industrialists eager to use and display their new-found wealth, with the result that it is easier for collectors to assemble services. Between 1730 and 1760 the bowl was made longer in relation to the stele and the handle's

16

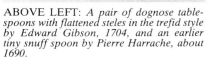

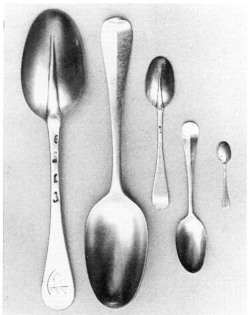

ABOVE LEFT: *A pair of dognose table-spoons with flattened steles in the trefid style by Edward Gibson, 1704, and an earlier tiny snuff spoon by Pierre Harrache, about 1690.*

ABOVE RIGHT: *Hanoverian rat-tail spoons, 1710-25, showing the range of sizes: table, tea and snuff.*

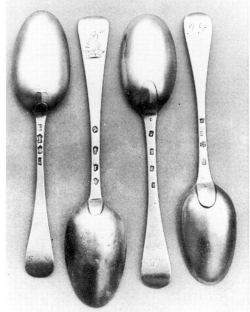

RIGHT: *Reverse sides of Hanoverian spoons showing double-drop (left), an Irish single-drop, and two Scottish variations on the right; about 1740-60.*

17

RIGHT: *Hanoverian flatware showing (from left) a spoon with a long central spine on the handle, about 1715; a long-handled provincial spoon, Dundee, about 1730; a short-handled, long-bowled London spoon, about 1750, and another about 1770.*

BELOW: *Hanoverian shell-back tablespoon, dessert spoon and teaspoon.*

central spine was shortened; later examples show how the balance was altered about 1770, the bowl becoming shorter and the handle longer — perhaps to conform with the Old English design (see below) which was, by then, superseding the Hanoverian. The ends of spoon and fork handles continued to turn up and crests, coats of arms or initials were engraved on the flat backs of the terminals. It had been customary since the introduction of flatware that when laying such spoons or forks on the table the concave side was laid face down so that the hallmarks (struck on the stem) and owner's markings, either on the back of the handle or on the drop, were both visible. During the 1730s some people appear to have preferred their spoons and forks to be laid the other way up. Spoon handles were therefore turned down at the ends and for the next forty years spoon handles turned up or down depending on which way they were required to be laid on the table. Fork handles turned up, with rare exceptions, since a downturned fork handle is rather uncomfortable to hold. The later design

18

TOP LEFT: *Rococo cast teaspoon, with contemporary teacup and saucer, about 1750.*

BOTTOM LEFT: *Three cast fancy-front rococo teaspoons, about 1750.*
BELOW: *Bowl and stem of a picture-back teaspoon depicting a domestic bird sitting on its cage with the words 'I LOVE LIBERTY', referring to John Wilkes and liberty, about 1770, by Thomas Wallis.*

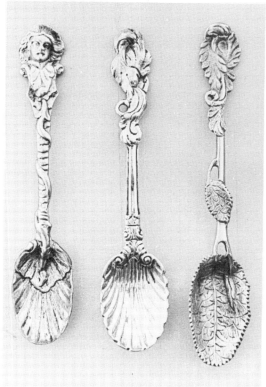

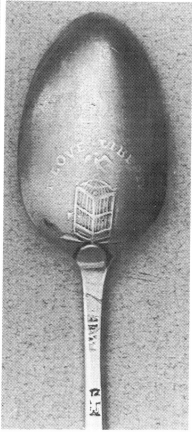

like its trefid forebear, followed those of the larger tablespoons. The exuberance of the rococo period also affected the humble teaspoon and, to a lesser extent, other table flatware. The undersides of spoon bowls were sometimes stamped with small shells, and scrolls and rocaille work were sometimes similarly applied to the fronts of the handles with an occasional amorino or mask. By the time of George III's accession in 1760 the scrolls and shells had been superseded by more adventurous designs. A fairly common motif found on the back of a teaspoon bowl was a galleon in full sail or a bird

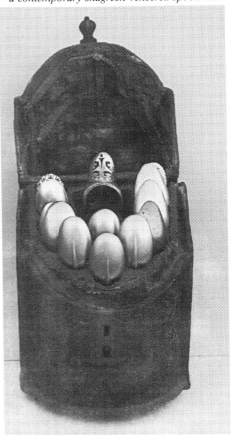

A group of eighteenth-century teaspoons with mote skimmer and sugar tongs, about 1750, in a contemporary shagreen-veneered spoon box.

Early mote skimmer (both sides), about 1710, the bowl plainly drilled with holes.

of spoon with the downturned handle is called *Old English* and lacks the central spine running down the handle, which helps to distinguish it from its close relative, the Hanoverian.

Teaspoons became commonplace during the mid eighteenth century since the taking of tea had become both a novelty and a luxury. The lines of the teaspoon, sitting on top of its cage with the motto above its head I LOVE LIBERTY, referring to John Wilkes and his views on freedom of speech (1768). Less common designs for *picture-back* teaspoons may still be found today, and some previously unknown 'pictures' have been produced by imaginative fakers.

An added refinement for tea drinking was the *mote skimmer* or *mote spoon*. A hostess may have used this spoon either to remove floating tea leaves from her guests' cups before she passed them round or for spooning the tea from the

Two later eighteenth-century spoons showing different styles of strainer: (left) by Hester Bateman, 1775; (right) by George Smith and William Eley, 1793.

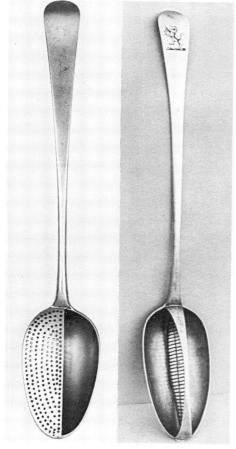

Two cast silver-gilt caddy spoons in the form of vine leaves by George Unite, Birmingham, 1850.

caddy into the pot. Tea then contained much dust, which was filtered from the tea leaves through the pierced bowl. The piercing of the mote-spoon bowl was at first confined to simple holes but became more elaborate during the rococo period as silversmiths became more adventurous with decoration and showed their skills with saw and file. The spiked end of the mote spoon's stele bears a similarity to the Roman *cochlear* and balances with the delicate bowl. Some authors have suggested that it was used for dislodging tea leaves from the grille of the teapot spout. Its actual use is still uncertain as other, much larger *strainer spoons* of similar appearance, complete with spiked finial, were made at this time.

The history of strainer spoons can be traced back to the Roman period, but few were made from silver in England until the mid seventeenth century. The first English type was made by drilling holes in the bowl of a contemporary tablespoon. The spoon was then re-weighed and the silversmith scratched its new weight on to the reverse side of the bowl. Eighteenth-century strainer spoons were made as optional extras to a table service and were largely used for straining lumps out of gravy. Either the spoon bowl was half-covered by a pierced grille soldered along one side of the bowl or a bridge, pierced and filed with narrow slots, was soldered longitudinally down the centre of the bowl. The bridges of later examples were removable for easier cleaning.

Another spoon associated with tea drinking evolved during the later eighteenth century. As tea was then a precious commodity, it was locked away from the servants in a silver or wooden caddy. In order to serve it more decorously, rather than just using an ordinary spoon, tea was put into the teapot with a *caddy*

spoon. The mote spoon became outmoded; perhaps its small bowl, which was less practical for spooning tea into the pot, and the introduction of a strainer attached to the end of the teapot spout solved the problem of floating tea-leaves. Caddy spoons first appeared during the 1760s as silver-mounted shells or short-handled versions of table flatware. By 1800 the makers had become more inventive, producing spoons shaped like a jockey's cap or an eagle's wing. Others were shaped as shovels, prettily engraved and mounted with pearl or ivory handles. A few Victorian silversmiths produced superb cast examples incorporating leaves or a fisherman holding a rayed scallop shell. Many caddy spoons were made by Birmingham silversmiths who are more usually associated with vinaigrette and snuffbox making.

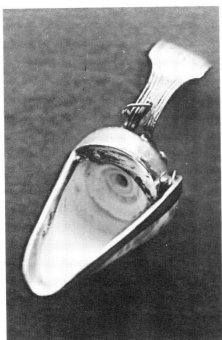 

Two Birmingham caddy spoons: (left) a shell mounted as a shovel, M. Linwood, about 1800; (right) an ivory-handled shovel by Cocks and Bettridge, 1804.

Bright-cut decorated mustard pot by Christopher Haines, Dublin, 1789, with a Hanoverian mustard spoon protruding. Alongside, a small-bowled Hanoverian mustard spoon, about 1740; a larger-bowled (more usual) Hanoverian mustard spoon, about 1770; a beaded Old English mustard spoon, by Hyam Hyams, 1865.

SPECIALISED TYPES OF SPOON

Spoons even smaller than teaspoons were made either as toys or for the taking of snuff. Dandies and other fastidious partakers no longer needed to dirty their hands or white gloves and some snuffboxes were apparently made with a small lug under the lid to hold the spoon in place. Other minute spoons were made in sets of six or a dozen for use as dolls' house toys and it is difficult to distinguish between single spoons from such sets and snuff spoons.

In contrast to the minuteness of snuff and toy spoons, considerably larger silver spoons, up to 25 inches (635 mm) long, were made for serving at table and maybe in the kitchens of the nobility. The first silver basting spoons appeared during the early years of Charles II's reign. The handles of these spoons were normally hollow, made from rolled silver sheet so that they would not burn the hands of their users. The large spoon bowls were frequently engraved on the underside with their owner's complete armorial bearings. Later examples show that the idea of a hollow handle, although kinder to the hands, was impractical because the silver tube would dent or split, especially if the spoon was dropped. Spoons for basting or for removing stuffing (a small bowl on a long handle to reach inside a large bird and normally used at the table) were forged from one solid piece of silver like tablespoons.

The trencher salt cellars from which diners had served themselves with a pinch of salt since early medieval times were superseded during the mid eighteenth century by salt cellars from which salt was taken in a more refined manner using a spoon, rather than with the fingertips or

23

knife points. Hanoverian salt-spoon bowls were normally shovel-shaped, attached to a short upturning handle, and were either left plain or ornamented in the same manner as teaspoons. Old English salt spoons with the more familiar round bowls became fashionable during the 1770s. The interiors of many salt-spoon bowls were gilded to protect them from the corrosive action of prolonged contact with salt. The rear of the bowl was not gilded, suggesting that the spoon was laid upside down on the salt itself or the edge of the cellar when not in use.

Mustard was served as dry powder in a 'blind' caster (without holes) from about 1700, using a long-handled and small-bowled spoon. During the 1760s mustard powder began to be moistened with water or vinegar served in a drum-shaped mustard pot. Mustard spoons are less common than salt spoons and are characterised by more elongated bowls and longer handles so that they would not fall inside the mustard pot. Subsequently both types of condiment spoon retained their basic shapes but altered in pattern according to the fashion.

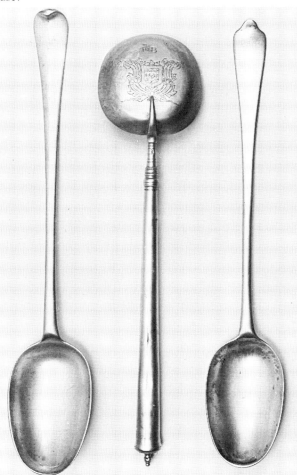

(Centre) Charles II period hollow-handled basting spoon, 1683, showing the underside of the bowl engraved with the arms of Burton and the initials 'F B'. (Left) A Hanoverian basting spoon, 1711, and (right) a dognose baster by Henry Greene, 1706.

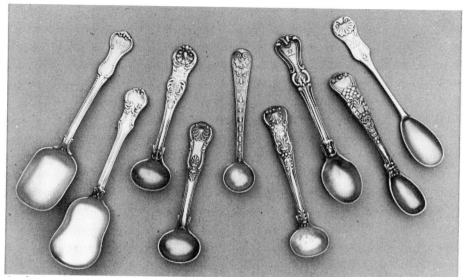

A selection of nineteenth-century patterns: (left to right) 'Princess Number 1' pattern sugar spoon, 1876; 'Victoria' pattern sugar spoon, 1842; 'Dolphin' pattern salt spoon, 1846 (the dolphins surround the shell at the top); 'King's' pattern salt spoon, 1831; 'Elizabethan' pattern salt spoon, 1890; 'Queen's' pattern salt spoon, 1852; 'Albert' pattern egg spoon, 1839; 'Coburg' pattern mustard spoon, 1840; Scottish variant of 'King's' pattern mustard spoon, Glasgow, 1827.

THE MID EIGHTEENTH CENTURY
TO THE TWENTIETH CENTURY

A further design of spoon appeared during the mid eighteenth century, apparently taking its name from a Speaker of the House of Commons, Sir Arthur Onslow. The *Onslow pattern* was based on the standard spoon designs of the period but was enhanced by a cast scrolled knop that was attached separately by a diagonal (scarf) joint, rather in the manner of an earlier knopped spoon. The longer-handled serving pieces of Onslow flatware have a particularly pleasing balance and elegant appearance.

Towards the end of the eighteenth century the Old English pattern completely supplanted the Hanoverian. From 1781 onwards the London assay office introduced a mechanical system of hallmarking using a stub of three hallmarks together. Since this was easier to apply to a broader area of metal, London hallmarks were struck on the underside of the terminal. Stem-struck marks,

moreover, were occasionally found to weaken the stem to the extent of forming stress cracks. Provincial assay offices followed suit during the next few years.

The discovery that silver could be fused on to copper was made by Thomas Boulsover, a Sheffield silversmith, during the mid-eighteenth century. Articles with the appearance and feel of silver could be produced at a fraction of the cost, particularly pleasing for those whose social aspirations exceeded their means. Sets of early Sheffield-plated teaspoons can be found although many have lost much of their silver plating. Larger plated spoons were less common at this time (about 1760-70) and were not made in significant numbers until the second quarter of the nineteenth century. Most nineteenth-century plated flatware was made by the close-plating technique. An article was made in base metal (normally carbon steel) and tinned. It was then enveloped in a sheet of silver foil and a hot iron was passed over it so that the tin and silver fused together. Silver on copper fusion was more favoured for hollow ware and both processes were used until the discovery and harnessing of electricity led to the technique of electroplating. The electroplating process was found to be cheap, rapid and effective and quality gave way to quantity as demands for plated wares grew. Electroplating was carried out on to nickel and wares were marked EPNS (electroplated nickel silver).

All types of plated flatware exactly followed the designs of their silver coun-

RIGHT: *Three bright-cut decorated Old English spoons, about 1770-80. The middle spoon is made from Sheffield plate with darker areas of copper showing where the silver-plated layer has worn away.*
BELOW LEFT: *Onslow flatware: two tablespoons, a serving spoon and a shell-bowled sauce ladle; about 1766-76.*
BELOW RIGHT: *Sheffield-plated flatware: (left) Old English table fork, about 1780; fiddle pattern tablespoon, about 1800; fiddle and thread table fork, about 1810.*

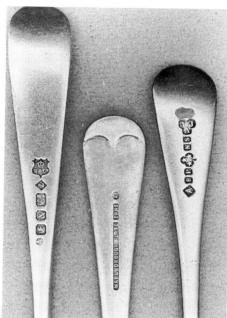

Electroplaters' marks including that of Elking-ton (left), about 1880-1910.

have been produced by Jacobites who favoured France at that time. The new pattern was a precursor of the well known fiddle pattern and is known to some as *fiddle without shoulders* but has been more conveniently nicknamed *oar* since the broadened handle has some resemblance to an oar. Another precursor of the fiddle pattern was the *shouldered Old English* which had been produced since the middle of the century. *Fiddle pattern* flatware began to grace southern tables sometime during the 1780s.

Oar pattern dessert spoon by Nathaniel Gillett of Aberdeen, about 1800.

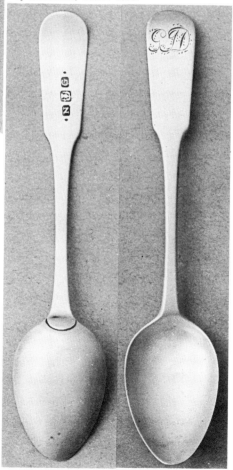

terparts; most were made in Sheffield, some in Birmingham. Makers' marks can be seen stamped on to the terminals of electroplated spoons in the manner of silver hallmarks, each initial occupying a separate pseudo-hallmark such as T B & S for Thomas Bradbury and Sons or E & Co for Elkington and Company. Some platers, such as Mappin and Webb, Walker and Hall and Elkington, were particularly successful and opened salerooms in London.

Old English pattern silver flatware handles were often enhanced (about 1770) with bright-cut engraving or feather-edging giving an added sparkle. A simpler and not dissimilar effect could also be achieved with the die-stamping process, patented by William Darby of Sheffield in 1785. Examples bearing his WD PATENT mark are, however, rare.

From about 1775 many Scottish and northern English spoons were produced with longer and broader handle terminals as a variation of Old English pattern. They show French influence and may

Scottish fiddle pattern was entirely different in style. It was made during the middle to last quarter of the eighteenth century and was used almost solely for making teaspoons. It is not a variant of conventional English fiddle pattern and resembles more strongly the designs of period French and other northern spoons — the Jacobites were probably cocking a snook at the English — so the handles ended in a violin shape. Scottish fiddle pattern should not be confused with conventional fiddle which when made in Scotland resembles the English fiddle but is longer and more slender.

The English fiddle pattern and the Old English pattern have become standard

spoon designs, with many variations and decorations added during the early nineteenth century. Of these the best known are *King's* and *Queen's* but there were also variations which sometimes combined with characteristics from other patterns. The permutations are endless. New flatware patterns continued to appear throughout the nineteenth century and most patterns were collated into a book produced by the Chawner Company around 1875. One that appeared about 1880, now known as *Albany*, resembles the Onslow pattern and confusion has often arisen between the two. Albany pattern was particularly popular at the end of the nineteenth century and examples can still be found quite easily.

A modification was introduced by Victorian silversmiths when the fashion for heavily decorated wares was at its height. Many Georgian and some earlier plain spoons were 'improved' (about 1880) with scallop-edged bowls centred with a *repoussé* design of fruit, and these are known as *berry spoons*. Some spoons that underwent this treatment were decorated in a more interesting way. The practice continues today.

Round-bowled *soup spoons* were not made until the end of the nineteenth century. The tablespoon, which had previously been used for this purpose, was now made slightly larger for use as a serving spoon. The bowl of the soup spoon is notably similar to that of round-bowled medieval spoons but the handle was made in the style of twentieth-century Old English fiddle patterns.

The art nouveau period (about 1890 to about 1910) fostered unusual designs from leading silversmiths and designers who followed the movement. C. R. Ashbee and the Guild of Handicrafts produced some beautiful patterns that have exactly captured the style of the movement. The best known art nouveau silversmith was Omar Ramsden, who worked in partnership with Alwyn Carr until 1919, after which he worked on his own. Ramsden produced many individual spoons as well as sets of flatware; few, if any, were engraved in the manner of his pieces of hollow ware with the words *Omar Ramsden me fecit* or *Ramsden et Carr me fecerunt*. Many of Ramsden's

ABOVE: *A place setting of some variants of the fiddle pattern, also a modern version of the apostle spoon (second from right) and a jam spoon (right). The patterned wares include 'Albert' (top) and 'King's' (on the dish).*
BELOW LEFT: *'Albany' pattern teaspoons by Walker and Hall, Sheffield, 1912.*
BELOW RIGHT: *A pair of later-decorated Hanoverian tablespoons (originally assayed in 1760 and then 'improved' a hundred years later), referred to in the trade as 'berry spoons'. Many collectors regard this treatment as Victorian vandalism. These two, however, are fine examples.*

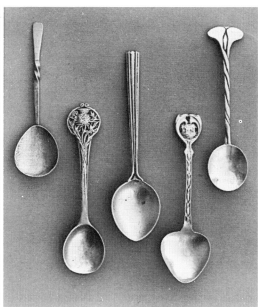

ABOVE: *(Left) An electroplated nickel silver soup spoon, about 1880, with an attachable guard for gentlemen who followed the fashion of growing a moustache, and (right) a group of art nouveau spoons by Omar Ramsden and Alwyn Carr, about 1900-20.*

BELOW: *(Left) Group of flatware by Omar Ramsden, about 1920 to about 1930. The mid-handle twist is characteristic of Ramsden's work. (Right) Novelty spoon by the Guild of Handicrafts to show 'the origin of the rat-tail', 1908.*

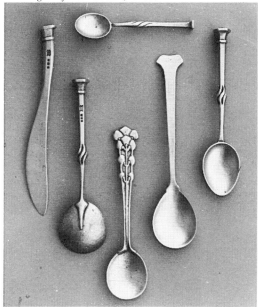
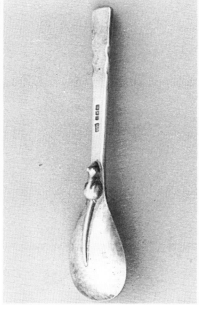

designs and those of other art nouveau spoonmakers were based on medieval designs and had a hammer-marked finish to show that they had been hand-made.

Plainer but equally unusual designs based on older patterns were produced by the Scottish designer Charles Rennie Mackintosh, whose flatware was also made in electroplate. Other items were partly enamelled in the manner of Celtic jewellery. The most famous of these was a range of flatware designed by Archibald Knox for Liberty's at the end of the nineteenth century (see front cover) and given the name *Cymric*. They can still be found although trends favouring this style have caused their prices to rise dramatically. These spoons and other flatware were either made to accompany silverware or were purely ornamental.

The Danish firm of Georg Jensen produced notable flatware during both the art nouveau period and especially the art deco period (about 1920 to about 1940). Jensen was particularly noted for original designs in silver flatware as well as jewellery. The renowned pattern known as *Kaktus* typifies the art deco style. The *Odeon* designs of that movement have spread to many other types of spoon, both in silver and plate.

Spoons commemorating events or holiday visits have been made since the early eighteenth century. Modern souvenir spoon handles usually end with an enamelled shield of a town's arms. Others use a motif to commemorate an occasion or the portrait of a famous person whose anniversary is being celebrated. Some have been especially commissioned for an establishment. Among the more imaginative souvenir spoons produced today are those of Milli Rich, whose designs are largely based upon old Dutch patterns; the bowls are sometimes embossed or enamelled.

Many people say that the designing and making of spoons has come full circle and that it is no longer possible to conceive new ideas without reference to the past. Despite a long and broad design history, the versatility and necessity of spoons may hold many surprises for the future, judging by today's imaginative designers and goldsmiths such as Stuart Devlin.

Georg Jensen flatware, 'Kaktus' pattern, about 1930.

FURTHER READING

Belden, G., and Snodin, M. *Spoons*. Walter Parrish International Ltd, 1976.
Caplan, N. 'Obsolete but Charming — Mote Skimmers', *Country Life* 175, pages 1704 and 1706, 1984.
Emery, J. *European Spoons before 1700*. John Donald Ltd, Edinburgh, 1976.
Gask, N. *Old Silver Spoons of England*. Herbert Jenkins Ltd, 1926.
Homer, R. F. *Five Centuries of Base Metal Spoons*. Published by the author and distributed by the Pewterers' Company, London, 1975.
Houart, V. *Antique Spoons — A Collector's Guide*. Souvenir Press, 1982.
Kent, T. A. *Early West Country Spoons*. Exeter Museum, 1975. (The Corfield Collection.)
Kent, T. A. *London Silver Spoonmakers, 1500-1697*. The Silver Society, London, 1981.
Pickford, I. *Silver Flatware*. Antique Collectors' Club, Woodbridge, Suffolk, 1983.
Price, F. G. H. *Old Base Metal Spoons*. Batsford, 1908.
Rainwater, D. T., and Felger, D. H. *A Collector's Guide to Spoons around the World*. Everybodys Press Inc, USA, 1976.
Riha, E., and Stern, W. B. 'Die römische Löffel aus Augst und Kaiseraugst'. *Forschungen in Augst*, 5, 1982.
Snodin, M. *English Silver Spoons*. Charles Letts, 1974.
Westman, O. *The Spoon*. Wiley and Putnam, London, 1845.

PLACES TO VISIT

Many museums have a few spoons on display as part of their local heritage. The following are especially worthy of a visit. Intending visitors are advised to find out the opening times before making a special journey.

Arlington Court, Arlington, near Barnstaple, Devon EX31 4LP. Telephone: Shirwell (027 182) 296. Good collection of antique base-metal spoons.
British Museum, Great Russell Street, London WC1B 3DG. Telephone: 01-636 1555.
Fitzwilliam Museum, Trumpington Street, Cambridge CB2 1RB. Telephone: Cambridge (0223) 332900.
Museum of London, London Wall, London EC2Y 5HN. Telephone: 01-600 3699.
Pewterers' Hall, Oat Lane, London EC2V 7DE. Telephone: 01-606 9363. An appointment is advisable.
Sheffield City Museum, Weston Park, Sheffield, South Yorkshire S10 2TP. Telephone: Sheffield (0742) 768588. Good collection of early silver-plated flatware.
Victoria and Albert Museum, Cromwell Road, South Kensington, London SW7 2RL. Telephone: 01-589 6371.